CHILL :

I'M MORE THAN

WHAT YOU SEE

By Chauntress Hill

Publishing Company

Wilson Paper Co.

1550 Wilson Boulevard

Suite 700

Arlington, VA 22209

www.wilsonpaperco.com

I dedicate this book to those who feel they must always keep it together and not let their guard down. To those who feel that if they are vulnerable, people will not truly understand. To those who feel they are perceived as weak when they shed tears because they are so overwhelmed. To those who may be fearful to speak up and truly express how they truly feel because they feel judged. To those who have a story to tell and feel that people may not want to hear what they have to say.

I am here to tell you that you do not always have to keep it together and I encourage you to let that guard down. I am here to tell you that it is okay to be vulnerable and open up to the right people because they will understand. I am here to tell you that crying is cleansing and a sign of strength. I am here to tell you we all have a story to tell and best believe there is someone out here that needs to hear yours.

A message to my readers:

They say that babies start learning while in the womb. We can hear our mother's voice when she speaks to us, reads to us, and even plays music or sings to us. We are fed through the umbilical cord which supplies and aids in our development. These nutrients help our minds and bodies grow. Meanwhile, the sweet sultry melodic tune of my mother's voice creates a song that transcends and finds residence within the depths of my soul that I will never forget.

My soul has carried many tunes as I have grown up. Tunes that have a perfect melody playing in the background, and others playing at times when I did not want to hear, or at times when I did not even want others to hear. However, each lyric, beat, and melody are unique to the notes that spill over onto the page. They are the notes that create my playlist as I rise in this journey called life.

For so long, I have felt that I needed to be strong all the time and not let people see the softer sides of me. I thought I had to be the person that everyone came to when they were going through things, being their ear; their comfort, their cheerleader, and putting the things that I needed last on the list. Don't get me wrong; I love to be those things to others because that is something that comes naturally to me. It's something that I'm sure if I tried, I wouldn't stop doing anyway. However, on this journey, I am learning to set some boundaries and learning to fill my cup first.

Acknowledgments

First and foremost, I give God all the glory, honor, and praise for keeping me along this journey of life. I want to express my heartfelt gratitude to my family for their unwavering love and loving me for who I am.

I am also thankful to my amazing editor, WilsonPaperCo, for your meticulous attention to detail and dedication to excellence. Your feedback and suggestions have elevated the quality of this work.

A special thank you to my love and my friends who have become my family-who provided encouragement, prayers, and cheered me on. Your support means the world to me. I am deeply grateful to each of you who have provided a listening ear and created a space for my vulnerability.

Lastly, to the readers who will embark on this journey with me, thank you for your curiosity and interest in my story. I hope this book brings you inspiration, joy, and valuable insights. I pray that my words will resonate with you in some way. I pray you feel encouraged to tell your own story because there is more than what we see.

With gratitude,
Chauntress

1 THE WONDER YEARS

You know the phrase "What happens in this house, stays in this house"?

I was born in Connecticut, but Joliet, Illinois showered me with memories of sunny summer days and endless hours running outside with my friends. I had a typical childhood. I grew up in a two-parent household with two younger siblings – a brother and a sister. Every summer, we would drive to Joliet to spend time with my grandmother, cousins, and friends. I can remember my first-grade teacher Mrs. King; she was so mean. Well, she was always looking mean and didn't smile much at all. From a young age, I liked going to school and getting along with people and I was always kind of reserved. I remember that every Friday they had breakfast at the school, and I would get waffles and sausage. Joliet was where butterflies flew by in slow motion until the storm came.

My parents both worked a 9-5, so childcare was a necessity, and during this time, I often went to a babysitter. It was an older black woman who lived in a big house. There was also a man staying with her, I was never quite sure if it was her husband or not, but he was always there. Other kids would come to the house that she took care of as well. She had a basement filled with toys and play kitchens.

One afternoon, I was taking a nap alone on the couch while everyone else was outside. I was sleeping on my stomach and woke up frantically to a man having his way with me from behind. I was too afraid

7

to scream for help. He didn't utter a word when he was done. He just got up and left me there on the couch. I sat there in shock, as a confused seven-year-old who couldn't quite process what just happened.

Unbeknownst of the traumatic and disturbing event that took place in that house, my parents continued to take me back to the same childcare provider. The same man, in the same basement, took advantage of me a second time, but this time he made me do things no seven-year-old should have to do or witness. He forced me to please him by performing an oral sexual act.

Afterwards, he wiped the remnants of his semen on one of the red play kitchen mats. Again, I didn't say anything, and I just pushed what happened down deep into my mind. I was afraid that he would hurt me and no one would believe me. I also wanted to protect my family's feelings. Mainly, my mom because I didn't want her to feel like she did something wrong with raising me. In addition, I felt that my dad wouldn't believe me. So, instead, I just pushed it down and kept it to myself. Being so young, I didn't process what happened. It was both molestation and rape, since I was forced to perform sexual acts (oral sex), and the other time, I was asleep and woke up to him on top of me.

Honestly, the details are still very vivid. If I allow myself to think about it, it takes a lot to get in the right mental space. This means I have to take some time and process what I am feeling by writing or listening before I move forward. Although I do feel that I have healed from that, I find myself triggered at times while I'm in a relationship.

A few days later, all of the kids were playing in the basement, and we were running around being silly when a table got broken. The babysitter got upset and blamed me for breaking the table. I'm not sure why she accused me, but it was not me who broke it. That was the last time I was there because when my mom came to pick me up she didn't believe that it was me who broke the table and had a disagreement with the babysitter. That was the last time I went to that house. I never said a word about what happened in that house. You know the phrase "what happens in this house stays in this house"? That's exactly what I planned to do; leave it in that house.

Dear Little Chauntress,

I hope that this letter finds you in good spirits. I want you to know that you are enough just as you are. Embrace your uniqueness and never be afraid to show the world your true self. Don't forget that life is a journey filled with ups and downs, twists and turns. Don't be discouraged by the challenges you face, and know that what has happened to you is not your fault. I want you to cherish the moments of joy and hold onto them tightly during difficult times. Always be kind, not only to others but also to yourself. Surround yourself with people who uplift you and support your dreams.

Remember, your worth is not determined by others' opinions of you. Also, remember you are not responsible for the behavior of others. Always remember to believe in yourself, stay curious, and never stop learning. The future is full of possibilities, and you have the power to shape your destiny. I have faith in you and I know that you will overcome whatever challenges come your way.

I met two of my childhood best friends in second grade. One of which I am currently still friends with. You know that friend who is always there, yet always handling life as it comes. The friend who you can miss their calls forty-seven times and when you two speak, there's no love lost, and you pick up right where you left off. That's my best friend.

I have always loved to read books. I used to read the Nancy Drew books and a variety of others. Also, I've had a love for music since I was young as well. I had posters of Lisa Lisa and Cult Jam, and I listened to the Jets 'Crush on You', my dad played After 7, and so much. Music has always had a powerful impact on emotions due to its ability to evoke feelings and create a deep emotional connection. Music allows me the opportunity to listen just and let it resonate with the emotions I am feeling.

Furthermore, it helped me understand and express my feelings. In essence, music communicates complex emotions in a way that words often can't. Its ability to tap into our emotions makes it a universal language that can help us navigate through various emotional states.

In middle school, I didn't have much knowledge of how to play basketball, but I joined the team. I was in a weird phase of going from adolescence to teenager. I wanted to be active because my weight was always fluctuating. I soon found out I was a pre-teen dealing with high cholesterol, so I needed to exercise and remain active.

My dad often took me to practice so I could work on my skills; he was more like another coach. My dad played basketball and he would referee all the time. So, he would always push me harder when I played and practiced. With him always there, I always felt the pressure of having to do well at it and not making mistakes.

In High school, I continued to play basketball. My dad would take me to the park to practice. There were times when he would train me so hard that I would cry because I felt like I couldn't breathe, and he would just keep pushing me harder to practice. My dad would also take me to the YMCA where I would play pickup games with men that my dad played basketball with. He said playing with them would help to improve my skills. He would always tell me that I had to practice and work hard because the game of basketball is 90% mental and 10% physical.

I felt empowered and challenged whenever I played in the pickup games. You know, there I was, playing with grown men and it made me play better and feel stronger. I felt seen by my dad because he always took the time to have me practice on the weekends. He would run numerous drills to improve both my physical and mental level. I still have a love for the game despite not playing much now. In addition, my body is not in the shape that it was back then to handle all that. I also ran track throughout high school, freshman, and through senior year.

Playing sports helped to teach me teamwork and I pretty much got along with everyone. I am not saying I was popular, but it helped that I was a part of something and did well at it.

2 PARENTS: UNRAVELING ROOTS

I understood the sacrifice, but it didn't take away my desire to hang out with my friends and be a "normal" teenager.

Growing up, my parents weren't particularly happy together. As the oldest child, I was always with my younger siblings whenever my parents were working. After work, my dad often did his own thing. Some nights, he would be out at a game as a referee, and other nights, he would be hanging out with friends.

During the summers that we didn't go to Joliet, I would be with my siblings because my mom didn't want to put them in daycare because of its expensive cost. At the time, it sucked but I did what I had to so I could help my mom. Even though it meant sacrificing time with my friends, going to amusement parks, etc. I understood the sacrifice, but it didn't take away my desire to hang out with my friends and be a "normal" teenager.

Although my parents were married, it was not always a healthy environment for me and my siblings to be in. My mom has always been the person to be there for everybody, (i.e., being our mom, and there for all of her siblings). Whenever anyone in the family needed something it was usually my mom that they called on and she never said no or set any boundaries. In addition, my parents often argued and my mom would be left crying, upset, and then having to take care of us. She always made sure we had whatever we needed and sometimes wanted. My dad was there but not as emotionally as he should have been.

As the oldest, I felt like I had to console my mom whenever they had arguments. I often felt I was stuck in the middle of them both especially as my dad would want me to choose sides and see things from his point of view. If I didn't necessarily agree then he would be upset with me too. It felt really weird sometimes because all I often wanted was to be there for both of them but I didn't know how to do that.

Though my dad and I have a good relationship, I have a stronger bond with my mom. My dad isn't always the easiest to talk to and at times, we bump heads because we both have a strong will and are opinionated. This trait results in us not always seeing eye to eye with one another. I feel like he sees me through the lens of when I was younger or maybe during my high school and college years. Also, he isn't very expressive when it comes to wanting that love and affection. He doesn't hug me or my siblings often. He is better at saying 'I love you' sometimes after we talk on the phone but it is not very often.

With my mom, I talk to her daily on the phone. I hold her in high regard and value her opinions always. Sometimes to a fault because I am an adult and I used to feel like I had to prove myself. Since I am the oldest, I am seen as the strong one; the one that they come to for anything. It can be a listening ear, advice, etc. I was the one watching my brother and sister when they were younger.

I never talked about how I felt as the oldest watching after my younger siblings because I felt they didn't want to hear it as they never asked. My parents were consumed with providing for us by working. Therefore, I felt I had to step into that role, so it didn't matter what I was feeling. I also learned back then that I could not show my emotions or how things affected me because who would listen? I know my mom wanted to do that, but she had so much going on that she didn't have the time to process my feelings with me. Therefore, I learned to just push them down and cry in the moments when it became too much. In those periods, I also turned to writing poems and reading books as a way to release and escape what I was feeling. Of course, I didn't share any of the poems with anyone because I felt, who would understand or care about what I was feeling?

On one particular afternoon, my parents were arguing. I can't recall what events led up to it, but I know my mom called the police and when they came they put my dad in handcuffs. I instantly burst into tears.

However, after it was all said and done, there was no conversation about what happened, or how to process the emotions I felt.

In another incident, my dad came home from work pissed off, he and my mom both yelled at each other as usual. My dad was upset and felt that since he purchased some of the groceries, he was going to take the food that he bought and then throw it in the garbage. He told my mom that if we wanted to eat then she would have to go buy the food. My mom was pissed and she let it be known. But after, she still held down her role as a provider. She often either bought more food or used what we had at home to make another meal.

Now, this is something that I and my siblings had to witness, and it stuck with me forever. The last incident that has stayed in my mind is that one evening we were eating dinner and my dad, again, was upset with my mom. He became so angry that he threw the plate of food at my mom, but she moved out of the way just in time. Food flew everywhere as the plate crashed into the wall above the kitchen sink.

Unfortunately, the way that my dad usually apologized for anything that happened would be to either pretend that it didn't happen or try to buy gifts to make up for the bad behavior that we witnessed. I don't remember him ever actually apologizing to my mom for what he did or said to her.

There was no communication between the two of them to talk through what had happened; it was just as if it didn't exist. I can remember my siblings being upset and crying but at the time it didn't seem to affect them much as they were still a bit younger than me. This continued throughout middle and high school for me until I graduated high school when I was eighteen, and went off to college..

I do believe that certain events that transpired in my life as a child and adolescent affected me and have caused me to push things down and keep going. I witnessed my parents' arguments but never saw or heard them reconcile. I didn't have an example of the proper way to express my feelings and emotions healthily. Therefore, in relationships I used to do the same thing. I would shut down when in arguments or disagreements. I would isolate myself to process my feelings before being able to talk with my partner.

In addition, I tried to avoid conflict. So I would often try to avoid rocking the boat in an attempt to keep the peace; which did not work at all. This would just lead to resentment or bitterness and then the feelings build like a volcano then erupt after some time. Therefore, I have had to find ways to process my emotions more healthily because we all know that when volcanoes erupt it can lead to disaster.

3 COLLEGE CHRONICLES: BREAKING CHAINS, EMBRACING FREEDOM

I didn't have to listen to my parents argue and I could do whatever I wanted.

College was freedom for me. I didn't have to listen to my parents argue and I could do whatever I wanted. I can remember that my dad was sad that I was going off to college. Even though I could have commuted to school, I chose to live on campus. I felt bad because I was leaving my brother and sister but I felt it was something that I had to do. My first year of school was an adjustment, I felt that I was a bit sheltered and then had a bunch of freedom. It was more like I finally burst through the door to see the outside world. I went to class, hung out with friends, and even joined the pep squad; where we would dance at the basketball games during halftime.

I can remember that when I was going off to college; my dad wanted me to still live at home and just commute to school. However, I knew that if I still lived at home I wouldn't be free and would have to continue to help out with my siblings. In addition, I would have to continue to listen to my parents argue and that is just something that I wanted some peace from. In the same token though, I was a little sad that my siblings would still have to endure their arguments. Yet I knew that they would be okay and so would I because it was about to be a great experience.

I met my college boyfriend when we were both working at Best Buy. He was tall, good-looking, had a great sense of humor, and we would have fun no matter what we did. We would go on dates to different restaurants or simply just stay in the house with friends to hang out.

I can remember a night I was at his house and we ended up having a water gun fight in the house! There was water everywhere but it was so much fun and it was so carefree. He also speaks Spanish and that always intrigued me since I had taken some classes while in high school but wanted to learn to speak it fluently.

Overall, he was very loving, caring, kind, and affectionate. He always had a great laugh. All of those things drew me to him. When I met him I felt like I was a little naive because I felt I had been kind of sheltered in my high school years so going to college was a whole new freedom for me. It allowed me to do what I wanted without having my parents watching me or telling me to babysit my brother and sister.

When I met him, it was like 'Oh wow, here is this man who sees me for me and loves me'. I naturally wanted to spend time with him. He felt safe and I felt like he allowed me to be myself without any judgment. I am not sure if it was butterflies, but I do know that I loved him and during that time, he made me feel happy.

During the holidays, I went home for Thanksgiving break, and my dad said that I looked different. I had no idea what he was talking about because at this time I didn't know I was pregnant yet. So as the Christmas holiday was approaching, I can remember being very tired and wanting to sleep all the time. My boyfriend then said, "Okay I am calling the doctor because we need to find out what is going on. This isn't like you." Right after the New Year, I had a doctor's appointment and it was on my birthday (Jan. 7th).

At the appointment, I was telling the doctor my symptoms and she stated that I should take a pregnancy test; however, they didn't have any in the office. So, she sent me to the lab to get blood work done. I was anxious as I didn't want to wait for the results and since it was my birthday I was going home to have a family dinner. During the entire dinner, I was not focused at all because I was anxiously awaiting a call from the doctor. We sat around the table talking about college, reminiscing about the fun summers of the past and catching up on life; but my mind was elsewhere. That night, when I got home from having dinner with my family, my boyfriend had written a beautiful letter and at the end of the letter, he said *congratulations*. It was then that it was confirmed, we were going to be parents.

There were so many emotions in that moment; happiness because I now had this tiny human growing inside of me. It was unplanned but still conceived with so much love. There was fear because I didn't know what my parents would say but I had a feeling that it would not be well received,

24

especially from my dad. I had some fears myself. Will I be a good mom? How will this relationship play out now that we will have a child to raise?

In addition, we came from two different backgrounds and were raised differently. First and foremost, how do I say, "Hey Mom & Dad! I've only been in college one year, and guess what - I'm pregnant!" I was terrified at the thought of telling my parents that I was carrying their grandchild. I assumed that my parents would be upset with me for getting pregnant so soon since it was my first year of college and I had just really started to be out on my own. I knew my dad would be angry with me and disappointed in me. When the moment came to tell my parents, I first called them on the phone to ease into it before going to see them again. "Hi, mom & dad. I'm pregnant," I blurted out. My mom was surprised but said that she already knew and that she was waiting for me to tell her. My dad on the other hand didn't hold back and let me know how he also could tell from the last time that he saw me but he was disappointed in me.

I wasn't surprised by his reaction and deep down knew that was something that he would say. When I did go visit them in person, I remember my dad and I arguing. He was angry that I had dated someone outside of my race; he felt that I was not going to amount to anything being that I was having a baby so young. However, in reality, I was not as young, I was twenty years old but I understood what he meant.   Needless to say,

25

I left my parents' house that day feeling defeated, hurt, and so sad. I cried so hard and it felt as though I was having contractions but it was way too early. I was able to calm myself on the drive back to my house. I knew that despite his anger and the words, my dad loved me. I was also more determined than ever to show him that I was more than what he thought of me at that moment.

My pregnancy was good overall, I have to say that being pregnant during the summer months is no joke! I definitely felt like eating for two was my excuse to eat whatever I wanted, and I didn't apologize for it. I can remember his mom trying to tell me that I shouldn't eat certain things, but I didn't listen at all.

I was still going to school at the beginning of my pregnancy. While going to classes or walking around campus, I always felt like everyone was staring and judging me. There was one class that I had and the teacher was so strict but I would always have morning sickness-which caused me to be in the bathroom vomiting and trying to get myself together. This particular day was not different and when I came back from the bathroom I had missed the remainder of the class.

The professor came up to me as I was gathering my things and asked if everything was okay. I told her I was pregnant and was dealing with morning sickness and I felt like she was sympathetic but also looked as if she felt sorry for me. I walked away with my head held high either way but needless to say, I did not return to the class after that. Once the semester ended, I had to put school on hold.

My due date was September 20th, 2003, but it was clear that my baby girl had other plans. It was a weekday, and I was feeling some discomfort but just chalked it up to being nine months. Throughout the night, I was so uncomfortable and didn't sleep much. I noticed some spotting and I was getting worried. I told my boyfriend but he just told me it would be okay and to go back to sleep which I definitely couldn't sleep. That next morning as he was getting ready for work, I told him I felt like something was wrong; so I decided to call my doctor. The doctor told me to take my time but to come in for an appointment. So, we took our time getting to the hospital, and even stopped at Walmart to get film for the camera, but there was still discomfort and cramping. Once we arrived, I was checked out and to both of our surprise I was already five centimeters dilated and we were going to have a baby! I had to call my mom because I needed her by my side, and she came right away. I will spare the details of that day but after twelve long hours of labor and some minor complications, I delivered a beautiful healthy baby girl on September 9th, 2003.

4 MOTHERHOOD

*I would do it all over again
to look at her beautiful face
and to love her the way I do.*

After eight years, my boyfriend and I decided to separate and focus on co-parenting, which we did well. Although we weren't together, we shared custody and would still host joint birthday celebrations for our daughter. When my daughter and I moved out and got my place; he was there to help look and make sure it was in a good area. We created an arrangement, agreed upon it, and did not go through the court system from the beginning. We were both mature and in a good space. Co-parenting started rough for me. I dreamed of marriage, raising a family in a two-person household, and taking family trips together like you see in commercials and magazines. But this wasn't my reality, not at this moment.

Being a single mom was not an easy feat. I struggled and at times as I was working two to three jobs while going to school. Working multiple jobs while taking care of my baby girl was not easy and it had effects on me physically and mentally. During that time, I was working the 3rd shift; going to work from 11 pm to 7 am; Wednesday-Saturday. My daughter was old enough to go to school by this time, so I was picking her up at 3:30pm from school; going to after school activities (homework, Girl Scouts, or extracurricular activity). Near 6:00pm/6:30pm we had dinner, took baths, then I'd drop her off at her dad's house. I would then get ready and be at work by 11 pm. Once I got off of work by 7:00am, I'd go home to shower, then go to job #2 from 9:00am to 3:00pm, then head to pick my daughter up from school. On Mondays and Tuesdays, I woke up at 6:00am to get us ready, then off to school by 8:00am, work by 9:00am and off at 3:00pm. I was constantly getting sick, and I was forced to slow down.

While many things have transpired through my journey of motherhood, however, I wouldn't change a thing. I would do it all over again to look at her beautiful face and to love her the way that I do. To be called a Mom, is truly a blessing and the best gift that I could ever receive. Motherhood has been a blessing and with blessings, there are also some challenges. While I am a mother, daughter, sister, aunt, cousin, and friend there have been many ups and downs. I have always had to be the strong one. The one that has had to be there for everyone while they vented or needed advice but I never shared any of my feelings. I would say that I have become a younger version of my mom. I always want to help everyone and make sure they are taken care of and I take care of myself last. I am one to always be positive and have a smile on my face even if I am hurting on the inside.

Becoming a mother has allowed me to refflect on my childhood and my relationship with my mom. As I look back at my younger self, my childhood I was afraid to tell my parents about what had happened to me because I didn't want them to think it was their fault in any way. I wasn't sure if they would believe me so I just kept it to myself and buried those feelings deep within the reservoirs of my mind. It worked while I was growing up; however, as an adult, it affected me when it came to having relationships, the very few that I have had.

As I was growing up, going to therapy or venting to someone about my problems, or just or just the thoughts that were on my mind, wasn't an option at all. However, I knew that I needed to find a better way to process my thoughts and emotions. I started going to therapy and it has been over five years now. My sister was the one who brought me to therapy as she was already in therapy and wanted to have family sessions.

Therapy has allowed me to work through my childhood trauma and has provided great tools to build upon as I navigate through life. Something that I've learned is that you don't have to only go to therapy because you have problems. Continuing to go to therapy is a check-in, maintenance in a way, and a form of self-care.

However, being introduced to the world of therapy was not an easy feat to begin with. I knew when the time came, I wanted to be in a healthy and loving relationship. In wanting that, there were things that I needed to address and heal from before that could happen.

I am very affectionate when in a relationship, yet it takes me time to open up. I also take my time when building trust. Communication is also an

31

area that I struggled with because I didn't always know how to communicate effectively. I like to be right most times.

In regards to trust, if a person does things in a way I think it shouldn't be done, it becomes an issue. It is hard for me to be vulnerable as I tend to fear that people will use information to hurt me or throw things back in my face. Through therapy, I have learned to be a better communicator and to work on trust issues. I am still learning, growing, and evolving.

My therapist always encourages me to set healthy boundaries. That looks like being able to check in with myself and being aware of my emotions. In the moments where I am overwhelmed or maybe not in a healthy emotional state, I should take the time to process those feelings. I've learned that I do not have to control everything. The only thing that I am in control of is myself, my emotions, and how I react to things. Therefore, even though I am there for everyone, I have to be able to let others know when I can just listen. I cannot "fix" people. I can be supportive, listen, and love people for who they are and where they are in life.

After holding onto my deepest and darkest secret for over fourteen years, I was ready to tell my parents what happened to me in the basement of my babysitter's house. Honestly, I was still scared to tell them but I had held this secret in long enough and knew that it was time to talk about it for me to continue on my healing journey. My mom was so upset, and sad, and felt as if she had failed to protect me somehow. That was far from the truth. I have always felt protected by my parents. It was a tragic incident that was controlled by a very sick individual. I didn't want my mom to feel that way and in a sense, I wanted to protect her feelings. For years, I was afraid of what my dad would say and that maybe he wouldn't believe me. Well, I was right. Not only did he not believe me, but he also chose not to talk to me directly about the situation and only conversed with my mom. I don't quite understand why he didn't believe me; as if I would make something like that up. To this day, my dad and I have never talked about it and my assumption is we never will.

5 SOMETHING NEW

Trust and vulnerability have not been something that I give or do easily.

Trust and vulnerability have not been something that I give or do easily. Even in romantic relationships, it takes so much time for me to build that trust and be vulnerable; which is not always the best. The few relationships that I have been in were draining because I'm the type of person who loves with my whole heart. So, because of this, men take advantage of me. They take advantage of my niceness as they assume it's a weakness. I have found myself pouring into relationships but never getting what I give in return.

I am pretty reserved and don't necessarily put myself out there to meet new people. Therefore, the people I've dated have been people I have met through mutual friends. Online dating is not my thing because it doesn't seem real so I didn't indulge in it. However, we are now in the days social media, so it is easy to come across new people every day. One day, while online and scrolling through Facebook, I started talking to this guy. Now, this was not planned, it was just an innocent conversation. At first, I was skeptical because one thing with talking with someone online is that you don't always get the authentic person. It's always like you are kind of meeting their representative, a version of themselves they want you to see and not who they are. However, I decided to talk with him more and get to know him.

With time, we began to talk every day and before I knew it, we started to occasionally video chat. I was living in Connecticut and he was in Maryland. This all happened at the height of the covid pandemic. He would come to visit me in Connecticut and I would visit him in Maryland. Things were going great and we decided that we would start a relationship. Remember that I had no intention of getting into a relationship; let alone a long-distance relationship while amid a pandemic. However, I felt that it was going well and that I was in a position to explore what this new relationship would bring to my life.

6 A FRESH START

*At times, I felt lost and questioned what direction
my life was supposed to go in.*

I lived in Connecticut for most of my life, and Illinois for a few years. I would have never imagined myself residing in Maryland. However, when I began this relationship, I decided to move to Maryland. I prayed about it and felt that it was something God was telling me to do because everything happened so effortlessly. I met this man and things are going well. I found a job and an apartment; so I felt like this was the direction or path that I was being led to. On the opposing end, my daughter wasn't my new boyfriend's biggest fan. She was eighteen years old and felt it was too soon for her to meet him, even though we had been dating for six months. When I met my new boyfriend, it was at the start of the pandemic. Therefore, there was not much to do, and everything was so uncertain.

Deciding to move from Connecticut to Maryland was not an easy decision to make. It was hard to move away from my daughter and my family. However, I found strength in knowing that God will continue to protect my daughter and my family. I knew that my daughter was safe, loved, and protected being with her dad and family. It also brought me comfort knowing that while it was a five-hour drive or one-hour flight away; I would drop everything and be there whenever my daughter needed me.

Looking back on things, my daughter never fully expressed why she felt reserved. Although, I do remember her saying that she felt it was too soon to move in with him as we hadn't been in a relationship for long. I think she felt I needed more time to get to know him. When the day finally came, my family helped me move and it was so emotional because this was the first time that I was moving away from them. However, it was bittersweet and exciting because I was starting a new chapter with a man that I had fallen in love with.

The relationship started well. That honeymoon stage was everything. Our individual "representatives" were still present. We would talk, laugh, go on dates and things didn't seem to bother us. We worked all day and felt like the evening couldn't come fast enough, but the nights went by too fast.

As happy as I was in my relationship, I still yearned for my daughter. After I moved, our conversations became shorter, and the distance felt like we were galaxies apart. Therefore, I did what I knew best, channel my thoughts and process through my emotions. I wrote this poem in June of 2021, my first summer here in Maryland. This poem is a reflection of what I was feeling while being without my daughter and away from my family for the first time.

Tears…

Tears are meant to be cleansing and wash away the pain, but do they really?

Do the tears I cry mean that I am weak? Do they mean I am strong?

At times, I don't know because the picture is so blurry

I wish my tears would wash away this pain that I feel. The hurt that has penetrated my soul

When the picture finally becomes clear and the tear stains are left on my face

What will I see?

As time went on; the honeymoon phase stopped. During this time, there were ups and downs as with any relationship. I started to notice some things within myself as well as what he showed me-the way we would communicate during conflicts, how we processed and handled those conflicts, etc. Everything was different. Notwithstanding, we got engaged after a year or so of dating and living together. With this new stage in our relationship, I knew there would be challenges so I wasn't really surprised when it all started.

However, I loved him and hoped that the relationship would be able to weather any storms. It could not. It felt like the clouds were moving in and as time went on, things started to change. As the days went on, I started to feel like I didn't know who I was. I had this beautiful engagement ring, a man, a place to live, a car, and everything but deep down I was becoming so unhappy.

At times, I felt lost and questioned what direction my life was supposed to go in. We started doing couples therapy, only because I had suggested it, and it helped for a while. Then it would go back to what it was initially. I would vent to my therapist and at times, to my one trusted friend but never really say what I truly felt because I didn't want it to seem as if I was complaining. Also, 'it could have been worse', right? Or so I thought. There were a few times when we broke up but we were still living in the

41

same apartment. We would then reconcile and then get back together. The only way I could truly express what I was feeling without judgment or questions was through my writing. Christmas 2022, I wrote this as it was a time we temporarily brokeup.

Late-night thoughts…

On nights like this, it is almost 2 am and my thoughts won't let me sleep

I silently think to myself, how is it that we got to this place

What started so good has now morphed into something different

As I think back, was it good or was it my mind stuck up in the clouds

On a high of what our love could potentially be, but I guess that's what it was…potential

The potential to be this great love story of two people from different places coming together

The potential of love being able to heal the broken places and push past addictions

The potential of walking down the aisle and finding forever in the depths of your heart

Instead, I got a love that used its words to puncture tiny holes in my skin

Instead, I got promises of things to come but never came

Instead, I got unhealed pieces of you and addictions that couldn't be healed by our love

I can no longer battle with the demons that you fight

I can no longer wait for your promises to become the reality

I can no longer accept the lies that seep from your pores to stop spitting their venom

I can move forward knowing that sometimes, good things have to come to an end

43

I can move forward in my truth and learn from the lessons

I can move forward and continue my journey of healing the unhealed pieces of myself

I can move forward knowing that there will always be a love for you and I wish you well.

January 2023

So much has transpired in these last few months

Words spoken, lies told, and hearts broken

What I once thought was a great love story, has quickly morphed into something ugly

What once were hugs, kisses, and intimate moments

Has now turned into cold stares, silence, and detached feelings

You are the shell of the person I thought you were

You spoke loving words, made empty promises, and no action

You disguised it with your laughter and mischievous smile, and I guess that was the initial attraction

Now looking back, it was all lies, deceit, and you taking advantage of me

My eyes were shielded, but they are now open and I can see

See you for the person you have come to be

A person that is no longer meant for me

What you once said you would never do, has now become second nature to you

You sling your words and threats thinking that you can wound me

You can say what you want because your threats mean nothing to me

You're all talk and we know that is cheap...

45

One of the last times that we got back together, I thought "Okay, we cannot keep doing this; if it doesn't work this time then maybe it is not meant to be." We were planning to downsize to a smaller apartment and begin the process for that. However, I decided that if I did that then I would be locked into another year for the lease and it would be difficult to break. I told him that I didn't want to downsize and he asked what that meant for the relationship and I explained as best as I could that I felt like it wasn't working for me. I felt that we were not in alignment with things and that I couldn't continue. Rightly so, he was upset and I hurt his feelings. I didn't mean to hurt his feelings and I truly did love him but I just knew that we couldn't continue this way. We broke up but were still living in the same apartment until we decided who was going to move out and where to go.

That time was torture because I was living with this man who I loved and he loved me but we weren't together. He was also upset and emotionally bruised. Some days, there would be this uncomfortable, awkward silence as we moved about the apartment not speaking and sleeping in separate bedrooms. As the days became weeks, it was only a matter of time before one of us exploded.

We both went to work like any typical normal weekday. However, I got home before he did and when I went into my room, it looked like someone had gone through my things. Naturally, I was pissed and knew that it had been him. Though I was unsure of what it was that he was looking for. Of course, during the time that we had been apart, he accused me of cheating and that I broke up with him for that reason. This was completely untrue. So, I texted him, "Why were you going through my things? I hope that you found what you were looking for." Of course, he denied it and stated he had not done anything. When he got home, I was still angry and again, I made the same statement. Well, he didn't like that and became angry. That was the straw that broke the camel's back. I will spare the details of the incident but I will say that the words he used stabbed me dead in the center of my heart.

Honestly, I have never seen him so angry toward me. With the way that things transpired, my entire world stopped spinning. My heart raced and I didn't know what was going to happen. During this entire situation, I was on the phone with my mom. I wanted someone to listen and be a witness just in case. Then I hung up on my mom because the situation was getting out of control and I called the police. Of course, it took what felt like an eternity for them to arrive.

While waiting for them, I left the house to get some air because my emotions were all over the place. I was so angry and heartbroken; not to mention I couldn't stop crying and I didn't want to give him the satisfaction of seeing me fall to pieces. I went back in to get my car keys and purse so I could just leave. My sister called and was attempting to talk to me and calm me down. He then continued to yell at me and accused me of talking to another man. He was still angry, and slinging hurtful words not worth repeating so I left the house to go and sit in my car. I called the police for the second time to let them know that he had not stopped and I needed help. However, it still took them at least thirty to forty-five minutes to get there.

As I waited, I sat in the car and now, all of my family continued to call- my dad, my brother, and my sister. While my sister was telling me to remain calm and leave the apartment, my dad and my brother were angry and ready to take a drive to Maryland to fight him. They also told me to leave and come back to Connecticut. Meanwhile, he had come outside and also went to sit in his car. I knew he was watching me. When the police finally arrived, I talked with them and they were no help at all. They pretty much said that there was nothing that they could do. After they left, he took off and I just sat there in the car and cried. I have never in my life felt so alone.

Here I was in Maryland with no family and feeling confused as to what I should do because Connecticut is five hours away and I knew that I wouldn't be able to drive that far safely with how I was feeling. In addition, I felt so tired, and weak, and my head was throbbing. My family wanted to come and get me that night but I was ashamed. My pride was in the way and

48

I felt like there was no way I would let this man run me out of here like that. I had to come up with a plan and fast because I could not stay in the apartment with him. For the next few weeks, I lived in a state of fear and fight or flight mode. I would sleep with a dresser in front of the door because I didn't want him to come in the room or if he attempted then at least, I would hear it. We moved about the apartment like roommates and hardly spoke to one another and were not in the same area of the apartment at the same time. A few times, he attempted to speak and would apologize. But I was not in a place to hear any of it. Sometimes, I would acknowledge him but that was because I wanted to keep the peace and didn't want another incident.

Finally, after almost a month, I was able to find an apartment, I called my family and they came to help me move. Upon moving and being on my own again, there was some deep reflection and healing that needed to take place. First, there was a brief moment when my ex and I kept in contact. It was cordial and very surface-level conversation. We used text messages because we would not speak on the phone. In hindsight, it was best not to keep in contact with him. While there were good moments in the relationship; there were also some bad moments. For me, the bad outweighed the good and it would not be beneficial to either of us by keeping in contact. In addition, I know that there were things that I did during the relationship that I needed to work on as well.

Overall, I felt that during the relationship I lost myself, especially when the relationship began to get bad. Ultimately, we just weren't in alignment with one another and the relationship could not continue that way. In the end, I felt like I was trapped and had to walk on eggshells but now that we had broken up I could fully breathe again.

Also, this time of reflection has made me think of my daughter and the fact that she had her reservations when she first met him. Thinking back, she probably sensed something I wasn't able to see and I didn't heed the warning. In addition, my daughter's father and I do not speak at all; so he doesn't know about anything that has happened to me. Honestly, I am not even sure that he cares.

Well, let me go back a bit and give a little more context to how the relationship is between my daughter and me. I was living here in Maryland while my daughter lived in Connecticut. With a very heavy heart, it hurts to say but we are estranged at this time. It started when I first met my ex, as at then, she was already living at her dad's house due to the pandemic. So, not knowing much about covid; she and I both wanted to take the necessary precautions to keep everyone healthy. Therefore, at the beginning of my relationship with my ex, I was living alone. The only time I would spend time with my daughter was outside when the weather was warm but as fall and winter approached, we didn't spend a lot of time together.

As I settled in Maryland, my daughter was angry with me. There were arguments and I have tried to understand what has made her so angry with me. I assume it has something to do with me moving. However, the truth is that I don't know for sure. Unfortunately, she has decided to cut all contact and communication with me. Sadly, we have not spoken or seen each other in almost three years. The pain that I feel is truly indescribable and it hurts me so bad. The best way to sum it up is that a piece of me is missing.

Over the years, I have tried to reach out through calls, emails, and letters. I have even shown up at her dad's house but she still refuses to see me or talk with me. All of this is extremely difficult to discuss because the feelings that are at the forefront are shame, hurt, heartache, and so much more. Of course, I want to fully understand how I have hurt her or caused her any pain. It breaks my heart that I am unable to fix this and I truly feel responsible for it all. As her mom, it is extremely difficult to not be there with her and to try to make things better.

In all of this, I have to be patient and understand that there are things that she has to work through. Also, I have to trust that God will work things out. God will reunite us when the time is right for us both. However, it doesn't get any easier and I feel so lost. I am deeply saddened but I get up every day and put on a brave face. I don't talk about what has happened to many people because it is hard to be vulnerable.

Although, it is still very real and a daily healing journey, I feel it is important to share. Also, while I am fearful and tears pour down my face as I write this, I cry out for my daughter. My prayer is that one day she will read my story and know how I was/am feeling. Furthermore, I want my daughter to know that she will always be a part of me. I include her in my thoughts, prayers, and all that I do no matter what. I want to share this vulnerability and take accountability for my part in all that has transpired. I love you always and forever, infinitely sweetie. Here is my message to you, in an attempt to express what it is that I am feeling…

My beautiful daughter,

As I write these words, I am acutely aware of the space that has grown between us, a space filled with unspoken words and unanswered questions. I want you to know that my heart aches with the awareness of our estrangement, and I carry a profound sadness for the distance that has come to define our relationship.

I remember the laughter we once shared and the beautiful memories that have been created; it is a bond that seemed unbreakable. Life has taken us on different paths, and somewhere along the way, we lost our connection. I want you to understand that my love for you remains unwavering, a constant presence that transcends any circumstance or disagreement.

I am open to understanding your perspective and ready to listen without judgment. Our journey together, though marked by challenges, is a part of the fabric of my life that I cannot forget or discard. I pray and patiently wait for the opportunity to rebuild the bridges that have crumbled and find common ground where understanding can grow.

I am aware that there are wounds that need healing; please know that I am committed to the process. I acknowledge my imperfections, and I am willing to learn from them. Life is too short to carry the weight of estrangement, and I dream of a future where forgiveness and reconciliation can redefine our relationship.

53

I respect your need for space, but please know that you are always in my thoughts. I hope that time will be a gentle healer, allowing us to rediscover the love that once bound us together. Regardless of the path we take, my love for you is enduring, a flame that refuses to be extinguished.

Wishing you strength, peace, and the courage to navigate life's complexities. I am here whenever you are ready.

With All My Love,

Mom

7 SACRED SCARS: MY HEALING JOURNEY

The journey entailed getting to a healthy space mentally, emotionally and spiritually.

I am now living on my own again after having decided to stay here in Maryland. While I have wonderful friends here, it is still an adjustment being far away from my family. However, I consider this as a time for me to rediscover who I am, what I like, and how I want to move forward in this journey of life.

The journey entailed getting to a healthy space mentally, emotionally, and spiritually. With that, I was still able to process those feelings in writing just four months into living in my new apartment.

It's been four months now since I have moved into my place

I was supposed to be counting down the days and in a different headspace

Instead, I've moved into this new season of life

One where you don't exist and can no longer bring me strife

I feel as though I can finally breathe and I'm learning so much about me

Things that were muted and so hard for me to see

There are storms that I must go through for lessons to be learned

It was one hell of a storm I was definitely concerned

As I continue to step forward, taking one single step at a time

Stepping into a season of what is truly mine

So here's to a summer filled with laughter, healing, joy, peace, and some wine...

This new season of my life is also about navigating the single life again. Honestly, this is not something that I focused on much. I knew that I had to do the work on myself before even thinking of getting into another relationship. I am enjoying this process of learning more about myself, digging deeper into my faith, and filling my cup.

As the summer begins to wind down, there is still so much that runs through my mind
This journey continues to be a revelation of who I am
Who I am without someone lying next to me at night
Who I am without someone to talk with or have my words cause a fight
Who I am with God at the center of it all, ready to receive my blessings even when I fall
Each day of healing looks different from
the one before it
Some days are the joy, peace, smiles, and laughter
Some days are filled with sadness, tears, grief, and other emotions thereafter
Each day that I get to wake up is truly a gift
Each day is an opportunity for my mind to shift...

So, what is it that I have learned and am still learning on this journey? Well, self-discovery has been about me understanding my strengths, vulnerabilities, and resilience. The resilience to cultivate the ability to bounce back from the challenges and setbacks but emerge stronger than before. I've learned to hold compassion for myself like I do for others and to remember that everyone carries their burdens, and we still have to show kindness. I've learned that showing empathy to gain a deeper understanding of the struggles that we all may face and be able to foster true connections with others. I'm learning to set and maintain healthy boundaries because it protects my well-being and promotes healthy relationships. I've learned to be mindful and embracing the present moments. I know acknowledging my emotions without judgment of myself and creating a deeper space of inner peace. The biggest lesson is forgiveness! Forgiveness is about releasing the weight of past hurts, allowing myself space to heal and move forward without being anchored by resentment or anger. It is realizing that there is strength in opening up and being vulnerable. It allows me to show up authentically. Also, the adaptability to embrace change and remind myself that healing is often a nonlinear journey. May we all remember that healing is a personal and ongoing process, and the lessons learned are unique to each individual's journey.

8 EMBRACING THE UNWRITTEN: NAVIGATING WHAT'S NEXT?

Overall, whether in love or just me, there is more.

While we cannot predict what will happen or where I will be in the next five years, I can confidently say that each day is a blessing. It is a new opportunity for God to continue to work in my life. With that, I can take the time to reflect on the progress and acknowledge the experiences that have changed my life.

I will continue to focus on trusting God and integrate the lessons learned into my daily life to promote lasting change. I continue to be open to new experiences and opportunities that align with the goals that I have set for myself. One of which is to be able to help others, promote change and encourage others. With that being said, I continue to seek support when needed from my heavenly father, trusted friends, family, or professionals who can provide guidance and encouragement.

In love, while I will not be having any more kids, I do see myself getting married. I look forward to sharing my life with someone special and the beauty of connecting with him on a deeper level in which the journey will lead to marriage. The lessons that I will take into the next relationship are continuing to understand my own needs, desires, and areas for personal growth. Being able to build upon my communication skills and express thoughts, feelings, and expectations unapologetically.

I will communicate in a way that is open and actively listening to my significant other. Establishing and communicating healthy boundaries to ensure mutual respect as well as understanding. Patience allows the relationship to unfold naturally, giving both of us time to adjust and grow together.

I continue to learn about compromise and recognizing the importance of finding common ground to foster a harmonious connection. Keep in mind that we each come with our history and flaws but embrace forgiveness to not bring that baggage into the relationship. Another lesson is encouraging personal growth for both of us. For us to be able to support each other's aspirations and development. Not to forget we will be a team. We will approach challenges as a team and work together to find solutions and strengthen the relationship. Having the emotional intelligence to understand not just my emotions but also those of my significant other is what fosters empathy and a deeper connection.

Lastly, to be able to appreciate and express gratitude for the positive aspects of the relationship as well as nurture mutual appreciation. Overall, whether in love or just me, there is more. Beyond the surface lies a depth of experiences, dreams, and resilience that is the true essence of being more than what you see.